BITS & PIECES

Great, wide, beautiful, wonderful world,
With the wonderful water round you curled.
—*Matthew Browne*

Those virgin lilies, all the night
Bathing their beauties in the lake,
That they may rise more fresh and bright
When their beloved sun's awake.
—*Thomas Moore*

So must your spirit become a tranquil and clear little pool, wherein the serene light of God can be mirrored.
—*Gerhard Tersteegen*

Down beside the tall, rank sedges,
Flag flaunt from the pool's green edges,
Fair, sweet roses haunt the hedges—
Laugh, O murmuring Spring!
—*Sarah F. Davis*

Came the spring with all its splendor,
All its birds and all its blossoms,
All its flowers and leaves and grasses.
—*Henry Wadsworth Longfellow*

Rapaciously we gathered flowery spoils
From land and water; lilies of each hue—
Golden and white—that float upon the waves
And court the wind.
—*William Wordsworth*

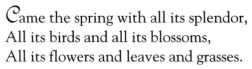

The spring is here—the delicate footed May,
With its slight fingers full of leaves and flowers.
—*Nathaniel Parker Willis*

Happiness is the light on the water.
—*William Maxwell*

The slender water lily peeps
dreamingly out of the lake.
—*Heinrich Heine*

Broad water lilies lay tremulously,
And starry river-buds glimmered by,
And around them the soft stream did glide and dance
With a motion of sweet sound and radiance.
—*Percy Bysshe Shelley*

Violets

Dorothy Cole Schrader

Do you remember where the violets grew,
Deep in the grove beneath the old oak trees,
And as we knelt there how the musky scent
Of violets and leaf mould mingled with the breeze?
We seldom picked them, only dallied there
To view their shy blue faces mirroring
The sky above; and then we wandered on,
Enchanted by the sights and scents of spring.
How many Mays we wandered hand in hand,
Thinking the one we saw was nonpareil.
How many springs we visited the grove
And searched for violets, I cannot tell.
But now a half century away
When I smell violets after springtime rain,
In memory I turn to you once more
Across the years, and we are young again.
Our feet are childhood light and we can go
Back to the oak grove where the violets grow.

The modest, lowly violet
In leaves of tender green is set;
So rich she cannot hide from view,
But covers all the bank with blue.

—*Dora Read Goodale*

Common blue violets dot the ground in Wisconsin's Devil's Lake State Park. Photo by Terry Donnelly.

MAY DAY RITES

Marjorie Holmes

When I was small in Storm Lake, Iowa, . . . April was primarily preparation for May. During April we worked on our May baskets with our hoarded supplies of ribbons and paper lace and boxes. Shoe boxes and cookie boxes and the boxes the big wooden matches came in; and candy boxes, those treasures already so pretty it was almost a shame to cover them up. Night after night we labored, with scissors and more little jar lids of paste, ruffling the dry crinkly crepe paper, rolling the tissue-paper flowers. Shelves and dressers became harbor for this fleet of lovely craft, and we would stand before it in a torment of admiration, trying to decide which was the most beautiful and on whom to bestow it.

On the first of May we dashed home from school to start making candy and popping corn. Mother would have already made a batch or two and at least one dishpanful of popcorn. "When I was a girl we filled our baskets with bouquets," she would remark. We thought this rather quaint and very dull—imagine not being able to eat the contents.

We were usually just finishing supper when the first thrilling rap on the porch would come, and we'd all hurl down our napkins to rush out to see who it was meant for, and try to catch the person who'd brought it. Then everything became a wild flurry as we tried to finish our own and steal off with them through the dusk. Sometimes handles broke and we had to come storming back to mend and refill. By then other baskets would have appeared, and the joy of finding them was

> *The sound of Miss Schultz's piano plinking away where it had been hauled out into the sunshine was lively, the scent of nearby apple blossoms was sweet. The colored streamers blew from the maypole enticingly.*

appeasement. By the time the stars were out and parents were urgently calling, those that had arrived usually equaled the number you had delivered. Though sometimes, to your dismay, you got a gorgeous basket richly stuffed, from somebody you hadn't even remembered. Or, thrillingly minus a name—which could only mean, or at least you hoped, from a boy who loved you madly.

Anyway, we stuffed ourselves on the plunder the way kids do now after Trick or Treat on Halloween; and for weeks the pretty baskets adorned our rooms until they collapsed and were carried out with the trash.

Each year nearly every school had its official May Day rites. A maypole was erected on the lawn, and gym classes did folk dances around it. The older girls got to do the maypole winding, an intricate process of prancing back and forth and ducking in and out in such a fashion that you braided a pattern of its pastel streamers.

I almost became a seventh-grade dropout, so great was my dread of this living puzzle and my approaching turn. "Don't worry, it's not hard, you can do it," people encouraged. I knew better. Some deep, dark knowledge warned me.

Practicing was sheer torment. The grass was green, birds sang, the sound of Miss Schultz's piano plinking away where it had been hauled out into the sunshine was lively, the scent of nearby apple blossoms was sweet. The colored streamers blew from the maypole enticingly. Other girls in bloomers and middy blouses gamboled about without a care, but

A group of girls enjoys the rites of spring around the maypole. Photo by Ardean Miller/FPG.

my heavy heart was in my feet. "Just take your pink one and circle the green, then back between the blue and the white—here, I'll show you." Miss Winters walked with me, patiently, in and out, ducking the blithe spirits dipping all about us. I was okay as long as she held on, but the minute she let go I panicked.

"To the right, now under, now to the left, now back . . ." I bumped into Aleda Womack, soaring lightly toward me; nearly knocked down Ruth Rydstrom. Even Ruth, all corkscrew curls and with the grace of a boxcar, could do it—she had a logical, mathematical mind. Despairing, Miss Winters finally summoned my younger sister to take my place. I was relieved but very ashamed. Worse, the dancers got to wear Grecian tunics made out of white sheets, and crisscross ribbons up their legs. I

didn't mourn the tunics so much, but I had always wanted to wear those crisscross ribbons.

Then at the last minute my sister came down with the mumps. Miss Winters didn't have much choice—it was either use me or call off the whole thing. She decided to risk it. I had no choice either—I'd already had the mumps. And maybe it was those crisscross Grecian laces, maybe the fact that Tom McCreery was watching, maybe it was the sheer singing beauty of the day—but I leaped about as nimbly as Aleda, pranced with the precision of Ruth, and finished the reel with only one slight hitch. By that time the glee club was singing "Waterlilies," and they were getting ready to crown the queen. I couldn't have been happier if they had put the wreath of roses on my brow.

In the Arms of May

Nora M. Bozeman

The arms of May are flower filled
With blossoms April showers spilled.
Bright, rainbow-colored gifts of spring
Arrived at her awakening.

The arms of May are sunshine kissed;
Her days could charm a pessimist.
Her flower fashions now unfold,
Revealing shades of pink and gold.

The arms of May hold springtime scenes
Of grass and leaves of lushest greens.
Oh, let me be a stowaway
And linger in the arms of May.

The May Queen

Alfred, Lord Tennyson

You must wake and call me early,
    call me early, Mother dear;
Tomorrow'll be the happiest time
    of all the glad new year.
Of all the glad new year, Mother,
    the maddest, merriest day;
For I'm to be queen o' the May, Mother,
    I'm to be queen o' the May.

I sleep so sound all night, Mother,
    that I shall never wake
If you do not call me loud when the day
    begins to break;
But I must gather knots of flowers and buds
    and garlands gay;
For I'm to be queen o' the May, Mother,
    I'm to be queen o' the May.

A May basket brimming with spring blossoms waits to be discovered. Photo by Jessie Walker.

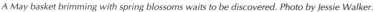

From My Garden Journal

Lisa Ragan

GARDENIA

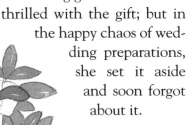

Gardenias are a delight to the senses. Just a whiff of the flower's intoxicating fragrance puts me in mind of old-fashioned romance like that of my grandmother's time, when a well-dressed gentleman sporting a velvety gardenia blossom on his lapel could be seen escorting his parasoled sweetheart across a manicured lawn. Gardenias possess an unmistakable, dreamy aroma that takes me back to a gentler, slower era filled with old-fashioned manners and romantic possibilities.

The most romantic story I know about this botanical beauty belongs to my friend Michelle. The story begins with a beautiful wedding. Michelle chose the gardenia to be the signature flower of her wedding; she used creamy-white gardenia blossoms for her bridal bouquet and even wore gardenia-scented perfume on her special day. In honor of Michelle's signature flower, her aunt presented her with an actual gardenia plant as a wedding gift. Michelle was thrilled with the gift; but in the happy chaos of wedding preparations, she set it aside and soon forgot about it.

Since Michelle and her husband were to reside in a small, city apartment with little gardening opportunities, her mother salvaged the gift and planted the gardenia in her own backyard garden. Much to the delight of Michelle and her mother, the little gardenia plant grew quite happily for several years. But, alas, it did not bear a single one of the creamy, aromatic blossoms that make the plant so irresistible.

After six years, something quite significant changed in the life of my friend: Michelle and her husband decided to have a baby. Little Grayson was born in the muggy heat of late June, and as if in joyous celebration of this blessing, the gardenia plant produced its first bloom on the very day their son was born. And what's more, Michelle's gardenia has bloomed steadily every summer since his birth. Ah, the mystery of life!

One of the secrets to the success of my friend's gardenia plant might be found in its planted location: the South. The gardenia can survive in outdoor gardens throughout the Southern states and southern California but needs the protection of a greenhouse in Northern climes. Most of the popular varieties are well-suited for greenhouse growing, both in size and personality, but some varieties (such as *Gardenia thunbergia*) can grow as large as ten feet. The best gardenia varieties for greenhouses include *Gardenia jasminoides* "Fortuniana," which will grow four to six feet, or *Gardenia radicans floreplena*, a dwarf variety that will grow to about eighteen inches.

Named for the eighteenth-century American botanist Alexander Garden of Charleston,

South Carolina, the gardenia has been grown in America since the early colonial days. Also known as cape jasmine, this tropical plant made its way to America from its native China and Japan. In addition to its distinct fragrance, the gardenia is celebrated for velvety blossoms that can range in color from creamy white to buttery yellow. The blooms shine out from a backdrop of dark, evergreen leaves that have a leathery texture and a glossy surface.

The gardenia is almost as famous for its difficult, temperamental personality as it is for its aromatic blossoms. It has a narrow window of tolerance for any change in temperature or humidity. This fussy beauty demands a day temperature of 70° F with at least four hours of bright, indirect sunlight per day. Night temperatures must not fall out of a range between 62° F and 65° F. The gardenia prefers constant moisture in both the air and the soil but will only tolerate soft, tepid water (preferably rainwater). When the gardenia roots have filled the pot, it can be repotted in a lime-free soil mix containing peat moss and potting soil plus sand or perlite. In order to compensate for its tendency toward iron deficiency, the gardenia must have a monthly feeding regimen of an acid plant food such as that used for azaleas.

Experts advise gardenia growers to mist the budding plant often but stop all misting when the plant blooms. Setting the plant on top of a humidifying tray of pebbles soaked in rainwater can also help satisfy its environmental demands. If a newly purchased gardenia decides that the temperature is not ideal or if it becomes stressed in any way, it will communicate its resentment by peevishly refusing to bud. Worse yet, it may even drop its delicate green buds to the floor one by one before the entire plant fades away.

Winter-flowering Gardenia jasminoides "Veitchii" is the variety most often sold by florists and has stunning, three-inch blossoms. "Veitchii," however, demands the exacting patience of a greenhouse gardener. The "Fortuniana" variety can succeed in the outdoor gardens of warm climates and blooms throughout the summer months. Southerners can also plant Gardenia radicans floreplena, which will form a low, spreading groundcover with small double flowers rich with that familiar fragrance. The gardenia can be propagated by taking five-inch stem cuttings from half-ripened wood in late winter or early spring. The cuttings will respond best to a rooting hormone and warm feet, which may mean providing a source of bottom heat to the new plants.

Two known enemies threaten the life of the gardenia: insects and novice gardeners. Insects, such as whitefly larvae, mealy bugs, aphids, spider mites, and scale insects, can be eliminated with environmentally friendly soap and oil sprays. Novice gardeners, however, are a little trickier to contend with. But they too can learn, through trial and error, how to please this finicky beauty. The above list of requirements provides a starting point on how to care for a gardenia but, alas, no fool-proof formula exists.

Despite the significant list of demands, gardeners willingly submit themselves to rituals of misting rainwater, monitoring temperature and humidity levels, and measuring plant food in order to coax those heavenly gardenia blossoms. I have heard that some gardeners, nearly delirious in their efforts, have resorted to talking, begging, and singing to their gardenia plants. I asked my friend Michelle why she thinks her gardenia plant has grown so well. She thought for a moment, considered that neither she nor her mother were expert gardeners, then shrugged her shoulders and answered that gardenias must thrive on the sound of a baby's laughter.

Lisa Ragan tends her small but mighty city garden in Nashville, Tennessee, with the help of her two shih-tzu puppies, Clover and Curry.

Gardener's Song

Sister M. Albertina

The earth holds healing for the human heart.
This joy I know:
To walk in paths where simple flowers grow,
To hear birds sing, to see the sunshine glow
While glad smiles start;
And this: to kneel and let the brown earth slip
Crumbling between my fingers, and to dip
My hands in hedges wet with morning dew.
Life's days are few,
Too few to work and watch the green things springing.
One cannot have enough, and time is winging!

Garden Paths

Olive Ann Pixley

A finger beckons me into the shade
Of winding paths that grace my garden-room;
One leads to summer-house for man and maid,
And one to that old apple tree in bloom.
A tiny pool lies in the garden's heart—
A silver cup, held in the earth's warm hand—
And standing by its side, an ancient cart
Is filled with seedlings growing in the sand.
A bird hops down one quiet sunlit path;
Another swings from top of apple tree
Then darts across the pool in hasty bath
And flings a carol to the world and me.
A garden and its paths are like a book—
To learn its secrets, listen, love, and look.

A stone path beckons visitors to this private garden in Allentown, Pennsylvania. Photo by D. Petku/H. Armstrong Roberts.

Very Lovely

Rose Fyleman

Wouldn't it be lovely if the rain came down
Till the water was quite high over all the town?
If the cabs and busses all were set afloat,
And we had to go to school in a little boat?

Wouldn't it be lovely if it still should pour
And we all went up to live on the second floor?
If we saw the butcher sailing up the hill,
And we took the letters in at the windowsill?

It's been raining, raining, all the afternoon;
All these things might happen really very soon.
If we woke tomorrow and found they had begun,
Wouldn't it be glorious? *Wouldn't* it be fun?

A Country Woman's Pleasure

Edna Jaques

A little sapling raised from seed,
A fenced-in yard where she can feed
A flock of yellow ducklings there,
A quiet barnyard broad and square
With a wide watering trough and well,
An old cow with a dinted bell.

A country woman has a sense
Of home within a sturdy fence.
This house and barn, this bit of land
Is something she can understand
As being part of all she knows,
A garden patch, a budding rose.

The pasture is a fragrant place,
Of meadow rue and Queen Anne's lace,
A little stream that wanders by
Reflecting quiet bits of sky
Where little newborn things can run
And kick their heels against the sun.

She knows the newly seeded field
Will bring one day its precious yield
Of ripened corn or golden grain
In answer to the sun and rain.
And all is part of her somehow—
The furrowed field, the scented mow.

Her simple pleasures and her toil
Are rooted deep in country soil.

A country woman overlooks her fields in THE CABBAGE FIELD
by artist Charles Courtney Curran (1861–1942). Image from Christie's Images.

HEARTBEATS

Isla Paschal Richardson

These things I love: a baby's worn-out shoe,
Stubbed at the toe. Soft shadows on new grass
In early spring; and cows that stand knee-deep
In shallow, shady streams. Smoke-curls that rise
From cheerful chimneys as the sunrise comes.
A jonquil vendor on a city street.
The sound of laughter from the children's room.
Swift, whirling leaves that fall with autumn's rain.
Bare trees in silhouette against the light
That lives a while after the sun is dead.
Bright restless white-caps flashing out at sea.
The floor of smooth, wet sand the tide has left.
The weight upon my arm grown heavier
As one I rock to sleep has closed her eyes.
The clean, wet drip of summer rain at night
Upon the roof. A winding, country road,
And shining pans upon a kitchen shelf.

*I have a heart with room
for every joy.*

—PHILIP JAMES BAILEY

*A quaint sidewalk flower mart tempts passersby in Troutdale, Oregon.
Photo by Steve Terrill.*

FLORIST

FLOWERS

19

TO A ROSEBUD

Dorothy Willard

Open, open wide
Your scarlet arms.
The waters of an April sky
Will flow upon you
But never burn you dry.
Rejoice with bird and song,
All that is springtime.
And, on Mother's Day, open up
Your red, red heart;
For you say the things that
I could never say.

MOTHER LOVE

Katherine Edelman

Such all enduring faith and prayer,
Such sacrifice and tender care
Are woven through this love; it glows
With all the beauty of a rose.
Yet strong and firm as rock or tower,
It stands in dark or threatening hour.
A selfless love, that man reveres
With greater wonder through the years.

*Pink roses spill over a white fencepost in Cape Cod,
Massachusetts. Photo by Johnson's Photography.*

Readers' Reflections

Today
C. Haney
New Brunswick, Canada

I must do my work tomorrow;
But today, my child, let us linger by the brook
And listen to it sing.
Oh, how lovely the pussy-willow kittens
That are borne on the branches in spring!

I must do my work tomorrow;
But today, my child, let us climb the stairs
To the attic and step into yesteryear—
Grandmother's old trunk is filled with
   such treasures;
The things she once loved we now hold so dear.

Today, my child, let us walk through
   fields of clover,
Gather wildflowers while we may,
Old-fashioned bouquets arranged in a lovely
   old crystal vase.

I must do my work tomorrow; but today,
   my child,
Let us make lasting memories that a
   million tomorrows
Can never erase.

A Gift of Gold
Donna D. Inskeep
Manhattan, Kansas

My mother gave me a gift of gold,
Gold like the Lord's sunshine,
Warmth found in her smile.
Golden locks, once like mine,

Found on my baby's head.
Precious memories, so worthwhile;
Family ties, done forever in a
   golden thread.

Editor's Note: Readers are invited to submit original poetry for possible publication in future issues of Ideals. Please send typed copies only; manuscripts will not be returned. Writers receive $10 for each published submission. Send material to Readers' Reflections, Ideals Publications, 535 Metroplex Drive, Suite 250, Nashville, Tennessee 37211.

Patchwork Memories

Susan Maree Jeavons
Rome, Ohio

I found it in an old house
In a trunk of treasures rare.
I took it home and carefully cleaned
The dust from each lovely square.
Then I spread it out and studied it
And wondered about the one
Who'd sewed each piece and quilted it
Until the task was done.
I pictured her with braided hair
And eyes of ocean blue,
And hands that showed the wear and tear
From the work she had to do,
Piecing it together from scraps that she had kept,
At night when she sat down to sew
And children finally slept.
Each patch was something different, a
    special memory:
A dress she'd worn to Sunday school,
A blouse she'd worn to tea, a child's old
    worn sleeper,
Her husband's old wool suit, her mother's
    gingham apron,
Curtains trimmed with fruit.
Each patch was something special,
A memory from the past, sewed into a
    patchwork quilt
And carefully made to last.
As I hold it in my lap and picture her back then,
I know she sewed this quilt with love
For her family and friends.

The Dancing Candlelight

William Edgar Kenyon
Monson, Massachusetts

I still recall the candle burning,
The flame dancing in the night,
Her old hands moving quickly
As she worked by candlelight,
Knitting or crocheting,
Slowly rocking time away.
Her face was like an angel's
With a halo of silver gray.

She'd ask me if I'd sing to her,
Which filled her with delight
As we sat there together
In the dancing candlelight.

I'd sit and play my old guitar
And sing her country tunes.
We'd sit like that for hours on end
While her love just filled the room.

My grandmother was special;
Her love seemed to have no end.
But she wasn't just my gramma;
She was also my best friend.

And though she left us long ago,
She is still not out of sight;
For sometimes I still see her face
In a dancing candlelight.

Contentment

Catherine Cate Coblentz

The sunlight makes a shining path
Across the room,
And on my window softly taps
A spray of bloom.

Your eyes rest where the carpet shows
A trace of wear,
And on the dirt small feet have made
Along the stair.

The wind sweeps in a fragrant gust;
The door blows wide.
Laughter and happiness and peace
Are all inside.

And you may have your Persian rugs,
Your stairs so white,
For I have daughters at my left,
Sons on my right.

Home

Betty W. Stoffel

If you have known a home that daily weaves
Its patterned happiness through those who share,
If you have known a home where loving leaves
Its spirit of contentment on the air,
If home has meant the heaven of all peace,
The resting place of heart's security,
The sum of every joy, the soul's increase,
The total of all good life meant to be,

Then you can be assured that home above
Will be more sweet than all your memories here.
For those who know a home of earthly love
Will only find the heavenly love more dear.
It matters not what kind of house or where,
So long as those we love are living there.

Inset: Small friends share a favorite story. Photo by H. Titus/H. Armstrong Roberts.
Right: A fenced garden welcomes the family back home. Photo by Jessie Walker.

Devotions FROM THE Heart

Pamela Kennedy

For we walk by faith, not by sight. 2 Corinthians 5:7

WALKING BY FAITH

Seeing is believing. I suspect most people today would agree with this statement. We want people to show us before we put our faith in a person or a product. Flip the channels on any television at any time and you can witness thousands of dollars being spent on this principle. A woman who once weighed three hundred pounds stands in a single pant leg of her old size fifty-two jeans, now a smiling size six. Before and after shots of individuals who are no longer bald, wrinkled, or out of shape flash across the screen. Seeing is believing, and the infomercials blare that message incessantly. But I have also been in the audience as a magician sliced his assistant into three pieces and made an elephant disappear! I know that I can't always believe what I see.

Although most of us like to think we can trust our eyes, the Bible reminds us that our physical senses are not the ultimate test of truth. There is something greater than sight. It is faith.

Gardeners know this—and so do mothers. There are times when the soil in a child's heart seems just as dry and barren as a winter field. There is no sign of growth or of fruitfulness. Indeed, the only things visible are a few stones of resentment and anger, some weeds of indifference, parched racks of defiance. It is then that both gardener and mother need the faith the Bible describes; faith that continues to water with prayer, to tend with hope, to watch with expectation.

Even after a child is grown, there are times when it is easy for a mother to become discouraged. Our sons and daughters don't always choose the things we think are best for them. They may not accept our values as their own or decide to follow in our footsteps. At such times it is tempting to remind or nag, to bring up examples that demonstrate (at least for us) the peril they risk by ignoring our advice. We can't see the response we desire, so we believe things are hopeless.

But I'm convinced that at times like this God calls us to move beyond sight to a greater place, the place of faith. Faith invites us to invest time and energy long before the first seedling is visible. It calls us to tend with gentleness the relationships we desire to nurture and to be confident that the harvest will come. Although it is tempting to try to hurry the process of growth in those we love, the result often disappoints us. Lectures and guilt-producing "reminders" only drive our children further from us and often destroy the fruit we desire to see.

Thank You Father for the gift of children. Help me to trust in Your provision for them, learning to walk by faith, not sight.

Walking by faith, believing without seeing, requires moving our confidence from ourselves to our heavenly Father who gives us the perfect pattern for parenting. How has God demonstrated His faith in us, His children? God loves us with an everlasting love that believes in our potential even when there is no evidence of growth. He looks upon our unseen heart, our dreams and hopes, and nourishes us with His Word, allowing us to discover His desires for us and manifest them in our lives. He does not wait until we demonstrate perfection before He sheds His approval upon us.

This Mother's Day perhaps it is time for those of us who are mothers to turn the tables and give some very special gifts to our children—the gift of believing in them without reservation, the gift of walking by faith in their precious potential, the gift of trusting in God to bring forth a harvest of fruitfulness in His perfect time.

A bouquet is colorful proof of a gardener's care. Photo by Nancy Matthews.

Baby Mine

Agnes Davenport Bond

Baby mine, baby mine,
What on earth is more divine?
What is there so soft and sweet
As your tiny hands and feet?
What is like your soulful eyes?
Who could help but idolize
Such a precious little dear,
Given to us to love and rear?
Let me hold you close today,
For the years that slip away
Will relentlessly intrude
And steal away your babyhood.

A Baby

Madison Cawein

Why speak of Rajah rubies,
    And roses of the South?
I know a sweeter crimson—
    A baby's mouth.
Why speak of Sultan sapphires
    And violet seas and skies?
I know a lovelier azure—
    A baby's eyes.
Go seek the wide world over!
    Search every land and mart!
You'll never find a pearl like this—
    A baby's heart.

A young girl relishes in her new role as big sister in A WATCHFUL EYE *by artist Viggo Pedersen (1854–1926). Image from Christie's Images.*

A
SLICE OF LIFE

Edgar A. Guest

DRESSING UP

When she was only three or four
She played at being grown
And oft her mother's garments wore,
As though they were her own.
She strutted in a trailing dress
And wore a bonnet gay.
For that was Janet's happiness
On many a rainy day.

She loved the game of dressing up
And having friends for tea.
The way she held her little cup
Was proper as could be.
For capes and robes and pretty things
She robbed both hook and shelf,
Took broaches, bracelets, pins, and rings
And hung them on herself.

I've chuckled many a rainy day
To see her thus attired
And have her curtsy low and say:
"Your company is desired.
A few friends I have asked for tea.
I've known them all my life;
And very happy I should be
If you should bring your wife."

Now to those grand and lofty airs
Has Janet fully grown,
And still her mother's trinkets wears
As though they were her own.
But what is more than silk and lace
And jeweled neck and arms,
She also wears with youthful grace
Her mother's many charms.

Edgar A. Guest began his illustrious career in 1895 at the age of fourteen, when his work first appeared in the Detroit Free Press. His column was syndicated in more than three hundred newspapers, and he became known as "The Poet of the People."

Sticky Fingers

Patience Strong

On the wall and on the floor.
Round the windows and the door.
Marks that tell without a doubt
That sticky fingers are about.
Round the place the toddlers sway,
Leaving traces all the way.
And houseproud mothers near to tears
Struggle to efface the smears,
Wiping vainly as they go

Paint that used to gleam and glow.
But though a lot of pains she'll take
Cleaning up the marks they make,
A mother's heart loves every one.
She knows how quickly time must run.
Too soon the little hands will grow.
Too soon the golden years will go.
But when the fingermarks have gone,
The memories will linger on.

A day's worth of delights are gathered in WAITING TO HAVE FUN II
*by artist Sharon Pedersen. Image copyright © Arts Uniq, Inc.,
Cookeville, Tennessee.*

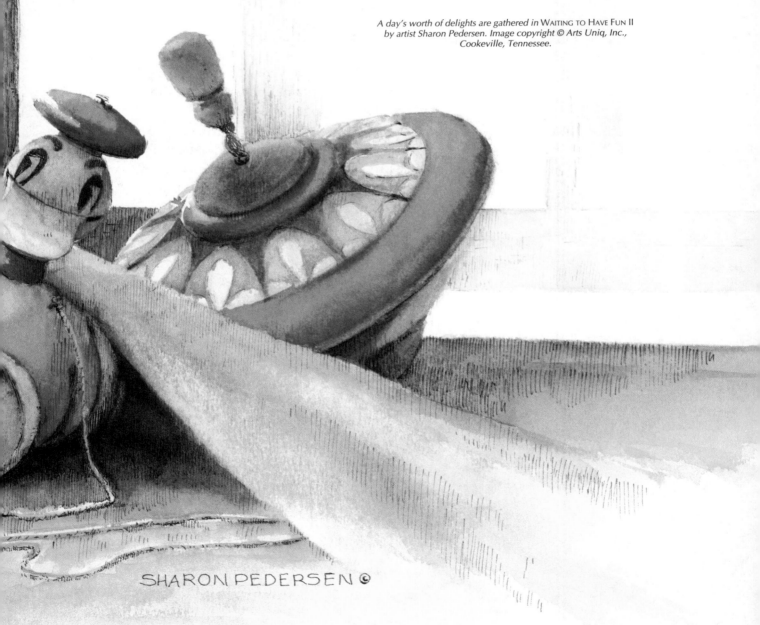

SHARON PEDERSEN ©

Sometimes

Margaret E. Sangster

Sometimes I think God grew tired of making
Thunder and mountains and dawn redly breaking;
Weary of fashioning gorges and seas,
Weary of planting great forests of trees.
Sometimes I think God grew tired of heating
The earth with the sun and of fully completing
The whole of the world! God grew tired, and so
He took just a bit of the soft afterglow,
He took just a petal or two from a flower
And took a songbird from a sweet-scented bower.
The dewdrops He took from the heart of a rose
And added the freshness of each breeze that blows.
Across long green meadows He took all the love
Left over from making His heaven above.
His kind fingers mixed them—God's hand and no other—
And made, for the first time, the soul of a mother.

A new mother marvels at her child in MOTHER AND CHILD IN AN
ORANGE GROVE *by artist Virginie Demont-Breton (1859–1935).
Image from Christie's Images.*

Spring

Mary O'Connor

She stains her youthful lips with wild strawberries,
Puts violets in her green and flowing hair;
She lays arbutus rugs beneath wild cherries
As trillium lanterns quiver in the air.

She dares the shadow-glooms to curb the spirit
And turns despair to laughter's rainbow light;
And gloom can never thrive when she is near it,
For she is promise rising out of night.

She puts her ivy arms around the hedges
And draws the world together, hill and streams;
She trims away the rough and ragged edges
And fills mankind with tenderness and dreams.

Fair Spring! whose simplest promise more delights
Than all their largest wealth, and through the heart
Each joy and newborn hope
With softest influence breathes.

—ANNA LETITIA BARBAULD

Wisteria blossoms drape an entryway in Oregon.
Photo by David Middleton/Superstock.

A Mother's Gifts

Mina Lone

I cannot give them gold,
These treasures given me by God above;
I cannot give them any gift to hold
But that He gives to all—
The gift of love.
Food I can give to make their bodies strong,
Strength for this day and for the distant year;
A home for which when far away they'll long,
A place of rest and freedom from all fear.

Faith too I can bestow
In God, in self, and in their fellowman;
And peace that comes from Him, that One divine
Who holds us in the hollow of His hand.
These gifts with love bestowed,
What more is there to give?
A mother asks and answers
With a life, well lived.

My Prayer for Her

B. Y. Williams

I do not ask for her, O God,
A brimming cup of happiness,
That fortune smile, that friends be true,
That she may not know pain and stress—
Just this, please keep her undismayed;
Let her love life, not be afraid!

I do not ask for her, O God,
That clouds may never dim her day—
Just this, that with undaunted faith
At evening time she still can say,
"For storm and shine, for calm and strife
I thank Thee, God, for it was life!"

To My Son

Margaret S. Roane

That your eyes may see beauty;
That your ears may hear sounds
That echo in light and love;
That your feet may walk softly
And with sensitivity;
That your hands may create
Something lovely;
And that your heart may reach out
And take unto itself earth's loveliness
And know from whence it comes—
That is my wish for you.
There can be no other.

A boy and girl rest from their adventures in this photo by Barbara Peacock/FPG.

To Dick, on His Sixth Birthday

Sara Teasdale

Though I am very old and wise,
And you are neither wise nor old,
When I look far into your eyes,
I know things I was never told:
I know how flame must strain and fret,
Prisoned in a mortal net;
How joy with over-eager wings
Bruises the small heart where he sings;
How too much life, like too much gold,
Is sometimes very hard to hold.
All that is talking—but I know
This much is true, six years ago
An angel living near the moon
Walked thru the sky and sang a tune,
Plucking stars to make his crown.
And suddenly two stars fell down,
Two falling arrows made of light.
Six years ago this very night
I saw them fall and wondered why
The angel dropped them from the sky,
But when I saw your eyes I knew
The angel sent the stars to you.

A boy dreams of flight in WINGS *by Kathryn Andrews Fincher.*
Image copyright © Arts Uniq, Inc., Cookeville, Tennessee.

Sewing chores become a pleasure with these beautifully decorated sewing baskets. Image from MEMORY CRAFTING: BEYOND THE SCRAPBOOK by Judi Kauffman, published by Krause Publications, Iola, Wisconsin, www.krause.com.

SEWING BASKET

Fiona Sinclaire

My mother taught me to sew. When I was four years old, she cut shapes out of heavy cardboard—ponies, kittens, castles—and punched holes along the edges. Then she gave me lengths of colorful yarn which she'd taped at the ends to make them stiff enough to go easily through the holes. She guided my hands as I stitched my way around those shapes, time after time, until the card-

board began to wear at the edges. Eventually, I graduated to a real needle and thread, which I used to sew together scraps from her sewing basket. I then progressed to pillows, aprons, and doll dresses. When I was ten, I was sewing from simple patterns. Mother taught me how to measure, mark, and cut the fabric, how to pin pattern pieces, and, when I was old enough, how to sew on her machine. It was a beauti-

ul old Singer sewing machine that swung up from the inside of a wooden table. By the time I was a teenager, I was quite skilled with a needle and thread, and with Mother's machine. I helped sew costumes for my younger brothers and a fancy dress or two for myself. I loved sewing as much as my mother did, and I loved the special bond it gave the two of us.

Decades later, I still love to sew. I have sewn draperies for my windows, covers for my furniture, clothes for myself, and of course, clothes and costumes for my own children. I have made quilts for all of our beds—some stitched by hand, some by machine—and even beds for our dogs and cats. Sewing is my escape from the demands and stresses of the day.

I have come to think of my sewing skills as a gift from my mother. It was her dedicated patience that saw me through those first imperfect stitches; it was she who patiently stood by and gently corrected my mistakes. It was Mother who professed excitement at my finished projects—equal pleasure at my first hand-stitched pillows and at the christening gown I sewed for my daughter last spring. From the days of sewing with yarn and cardboard to the present, sewing has been a wonderful, important part of my life, thanks to Mom.

When I came across instructions for decorated sewing baskets and boxes in a craft magazine, I knew I'd found just the right Mother's Day gift. One thing Mom always reminded me to do was save my sewing odds and ends—buttons, bits of ribbon, lace trim. She told me to keep my needles and thimbles in a safe place, to keep them organized and handy. She had an old cigar box to hold her sewing things. In that worn blue and white box she kept a red pin cushion covered with a rainbow of pins and needles of every size, her favorite pair of sharp scissors, her cloth measuring tape, and various other sewing essentials. I always kidded her about the cigar box, but she never saw the need for anything fancier.

And that is what makes my sewing basket such a nice gift for Mother. It is something she would never think she needed, something she likely would never take the time to make for herself; in fact, if I had showed her a picture of this sewing basket she would have said, "Oh, that's nice, but I *have* a sewing box." But she won't be able to refuse a gift from her daughter; and, once the basket is in her house, I know she will enjoy keeping her sewing objects in it.

I started my project by purchasing a sewing basket with a plain muslin-covered lid from a craft store. My basket came already lined with a soft yellow satin. It is about eight inches wide and six inches deep. To decorate it, I gathered a collection of items, some store-bought, others salvaged from my own sewing basket. I made borders on the basket's lid with widths of ribbon; then I glued on a pretty oval lace doily. After the lace was in place, I used buttons and sequins and plastic jewels to highlight the corners and brighten the lid. I also used a set of gold buttons which have been in my button box for years, awaiting just the right project.

A sewing box or basket is a project adaptable to any skill level, and it can be as elaborate or as simple as you like. I purchased my basket already covered and lined, but more ambitious crafters could start closer to scratch and customize a box inside and out. A padded basket top could be decorated with silk-ribbon embroidery or a piece of patchwork; a wooden box could be adorned with a decoupaged collage of old patterns. The options for decorating are unlimited.

A sewing basket or box makes a nice child's project too. Let your young one have free reign in gluing special objects to the basket's lid—collected buttons, sparkling jewels, even pretty rocks or shells. A kid-made sewing box would make a lovely gift for a grandmother or favorite aunt or for anyone special who loves to sew. These baskets and boxes also make unique gifts for children just learning to sew. Having a special box for sewing tools and trims makes learning the craft more exciting to a child.

I finished my mother's sewing basket in one quiet afternoon while the rest of the family was out. It was not a craft that took any great investment of time, nor did it require much skill. But it made me happy to work on it. I thought of Mother and of our early sewing lessons. It will not be the most spectacular Mother's Day gift she'll receive, I am sure, but it is one that I know will bring her pleasure as she goes about her sewing.

ELIAS HOWE

While watching his wife sew one evening during the early 1840s, Elias Howe came upon the idea that would consume his thoughts and energy for the remainder of his life and bring about a revolution in the business of sewing. Howe, a machinist by trade, had for many years dreamed of creating a machine for sewing. He had toyed with designs for machines that imitated the movement of the human sewer; but inspiration had proven elusive until this night. Watching his wife's expert hands moving needle and thread through fabric, observing the fluid grace of her repetitive motions, Howe realized that no machine could possibly sew in the manner of an accomplished seamstress. A sewing machine, Howe decided, must use a different means to get at the common end of securely attaching two pieces of fabric with thread.

Howe envisioned a sewing machine that joined thread from two sources—one on top of the fabric, the other beneath—to create each stitch. This breakthrough in thinking filled Howe with enthusiasm and anticipation. Believing the creation of a sewing machine to be an attainable goal, Howe left his job and moved his family into his father's home to lighten his financial burden. He forged ahead with his work on the sewing machine with great confidence, unaware that great trials lay ahead on the road to creating, perfecting, and marketing his invention.

Elias Howe was not the first to envision a machine to do the work of hand sewing. Howe came upon the idea while working in a watchmaker's shop in Cambridge, Massachusetts; but by that time other inventors had been at work on the project for fifty years. Most early attempts at making the sewing machine were mechanical failures. Others were defeated by social forces. A French inventor produced a workable design in the 1830s; but before he could make any headway in production and marketing, his factory and machines were destroyed by French tailors who had banded together to halt the machine they feared would destroy their jobs. Another inventor, this one American, had made progress on a sewing machine as well, only to abandon it himself because he feared the machine's potential effects on employment of tailors and other hand sewers. But Howe, encouraged by his employer at the watch shop who spoke of the sewing machine as an inventor's ticket to fame and fortune, was determined to make the machine a reality.

Elias Howe had been working around fabric and machines since he was sixteen years old and apprenticed to a textile mill. He was born on July 9, 1819, in the small town of Spencer, Massachusetts, and spent his early childhood years helping out at the family farm and gristmill. His apprenticeship took him east to the city of Lowell, Massachusetts. In the late 1830s, Howe moved to Cambridge, just

across the Charles River from Boston, and took a job at the watchmaking shop of Ari Davis. It was there that he first began to think about inventing a sewing machine.

When Howe began serious work on his invention, he had much at stake. So strongly did he believe in his idea that he had given up his employment and put his family's financial future at risk. Fortunately, Howe's idea for the sewing machine proved a sound one. With a needle and shuttle working in harmony on opposing sides of the fabric to create a secure lockstitch, Howe's machine sewed quickly and reliably. He faced, however, a rocky road from the perfection of his design to the fortune he had imagined. A fire in his workshop delayed his progress, as did the exorbitant cost of his early machines. Although his sewing machines proved five times faster than hand sewing, their three-hundred-dollar price tag placed them far out of reach of the average American family's budget. Howe secured an American patent for his machine in 1846 and then, frustrated with his lack of success in the American market, he traveled to London. England proved only slightly more welcoming to the inventor. He found an interested partner, but was eventually swindled out of his patent rights in England and left penniless. Demoralized by his experience in England, Howe used the last of his money to pay for his family's passage back to the United States and wondered whether his dream of a sewing machine would ever become reality.

What Howe found upon his return to America must have both heartened and horrified him. Elias Howe arrived home in the United States to find that the sewing machine had indeed finally begun to catch on with the American public. But he also found that other inventors had borrowed his idea for the lockstitch machine and had begun producing their own product. The most successful of these was made by a man named Isaac Singer. Singer's machine was different from Howe's in important ways. Whereas Howe's needle moved in a side to side direction, Singer's moved in the up and down fashion of today's sewing machines; and whereas Howe had used a hand crank mechanism to move the needle and shuttle, Singer's machines were moved by a treadle. Differences aside, Howe believed that Singer had violated his patent. Unwilling to surrender the future of his ideas to another inventor, Howe mortgaged his family's farm to raise money for legal fees and took his case to court.

Howe faced a long and difficult battle to protect his patent. In the end he was vindicated, but it was not until 1854 that the courts ruled in his favor and ordered Isaac Singer to pay thousands of dollars in back royalties. Two years later another group of inventors was required to pay fees to Howe for the innovations they had unlawfully copied. From the royalties that followed these two verdicts, Howe eventually made nearly two million dollars, a fortune beyond what he could have dreamed possible. His gamble had paid off; the Howe family was financially secure and the sewing machine was a lasting success.

The sewing machine was truly every bit as revolutionary an invention as Elias Howe had envisioned it to be. Sewing machines—stitching at five times the rate of the best hand sewers—made possible the mass production of clothing and other sewn products; and they also changed the nature of sewing for the individual home sewer, freeing time that had once been consumed by tedious handstitching. But for Elias Howe, success was not entirely what he had expected it to be. The long years of hard work on his machine, his tireless and often disappointing efforts to market it, and the protracted and costly legal battle to protect his patent had taken a toll on Howe's health. He died in 1867 at the age of forty-eight. Although the courts had ruled that Howe was the rightful patent owner for the original lockstitch sewing machine, his legacy would be forever clouded by the dispute of his patent. To this day, more people know the name of Isaac Singer in connection with the origin of the sewing machine than that of Elias Howe.

But Elias Howe deserves his place in history. Although other inventors played important roles in the development of the sewing machine and each deserves his own measure of recognition, it was Elias Howe's moment of inspiration on that quiet evening as he watched his wife sew that set the wheels in motion and led to a great American innovation.

The Charm String

Ruth B. Field

In Grandmother's button box treasures lay,
Buttons of every shape and size
Clipped from garments of yesterday,
Many just commonplace, some to prize.

Little girls many an hour spent
Sorting out buttons in bright array,
A pleasant pastime that always lent
Brightness to even a stormy day.

Often old buttons they would string
Shining and gay in a dangling row
As an old-time song they'd sometimes sing,
Watching their charm string grow and grow.

Pie crust buttons, pewter and pearl.
Mother Goose pictures, a castle, birds,
Lusters and jewels to please a girl
And a Greenaway child too sweet for words.

A uniform button from Uncle Jim,
Cut steel that once graced a velvet gown,
Metal rim holding a tiny type dim—
One by one on the string slipped down.

Here painstakingly long ago
The charm string grew, and still it gleams
With old-time buttons in jumbled row—
Strung with patience and a young girl's dreams.

*Inset and border: Vintage spools and buttons are reminders of
sewing baskets of yesteryear. Photos by Jessie Walker.*

MACKINAC ISLAND, MICHIGAN

Elizabeth Bonner Kea

I have a friend who, since she was a young girl, had her wedding planned down to the last detail. "It will be on an island in the spring," she would always tell me, "June to be exact, in a small church set among hundreds and hundreds of lilacs." I would tease her, telling her no such idyllic setting existed, but she persistently responded it did, that she had vacationed there once when she was very young, and it was beautiful. After we were graduated from college, I lost track of my friend, until one day I received a wedding invitation requesting the honor of my presence at a ceremony to be held in June at Saint Anne's Church on Mackinac Island, Michigan. I read the invitation slowly, and I began to put it all together: the church . . . on the island . . . in spring. I smiled as I realized perhaps my friend's fairyland actually existed—only the lilacs remained to be seen.

I decided to arrive on the island a day early, before the other wedding guests, in order to explore this place of which my friend had raved. I traveled the final leg by ferry, for no automobile is permitted on the island. As the small boat approached the harbor, I watched the sun shimmer on Lake Huron's water and breathed in the pristine air that carried a hint of floral fragrance. Curiously, I looked toward the island for the source of the fragrance and saw clusters of purple, pink, and white dotting Mackinac's lush green backdrop. Lilacs, I thought to myself, hundreds and hundreds of lilacs. Realizing my wonder at the beautiful colors, an older lady seated next to me commented, "Aren't they lovely? You picked a wonderful time to come to the island. I've been coming here nearly every May or June for as long as I can remember—just to see the lilacs. In fact, this will mark my twentieth lilac festival!" I told her my reason for coming, and she proceeded to inform me of all the attractions I needed to see while I was here. We chatted until the boat docked and we went our separate ways.

I checked into my room at the Harbor View Inn; and after a leisurely lunch, during which I watched the ferries and sailboats come and go, I strolled into Mackinac's village to join in the lilac festival. A men's quartet was singing down the street at Windermere Point; in the distance, I could see children flying kites in Marquette Park; and artists were displaying and autographing their work along the sidewalk. A spirit of celebration pervaded the quiet island. People walked, biked, and rode in horse-drawn carriages, savoring the Victorian ambience of Mackinac and enjoying the shops and events. And over it all, the lilacs presided—more than one hundred varieties scattered around cottages and in parks across the small island. They were displayed as bouquets on tearoom tables, crowns adorning taxi-horses, and in colorful planters set out on old front porches.

By the time the other wedding guests arrived the next day, I felt as though Mackinac Island had become my very own. By bike and by horse-drawn trolley, I had explored every trail and pathway I could find and now understood why, even as a young child, this place had made an impression on my friend. In my limited time, I had been able to see Fort Mackinac, a strategic site during the Revolutionary War and War of 1812; hundreds of colorful live butterflies at the Butterfly House; and the beautiful Grand Hotel, which dates from the late 1800s. Time had a way of standing still here. Perhaps it was the slower pace of life or the intoxicating fragrance of the lilacs, but whatever the case, I had discovered one of America's jewels.

After the wedding ceremony that evening, I

Vibrant lilac bushes grace the landscape on Mackinac Island. Image by Terry W. Phipps.

spent a few moments with my newly-wed friend, congratulating her on her marriage. She thanked me graciously, but then responded, "Wasn't I right? The fairyland really does exist, doesn't it?" I smiled sheepishly, "Yes, Mackinac Island is beautiful, and you were right about everything . . . even the lilacs."

OLD WOMAN PIECING A QUILT

Jessie Merle Franklin

She still creates with bits of colored cloth
Like unset jewels in her hands, and she
The jeweler. Now her joy of giving life
Is gone, but with it also went the pain;
And as all things created take the form
Of their creator, so her finished quilt
Will be both strong and lovely, so that child
And grandchild will admire it as each vies
To call it his.

Vaguely they understand
The memories she sews in it with her neat
And flawless stitches as she bears the shawl
Of years upon her back; but do they guess
The dreams she sews? A mortal must dream on,
It seems, to live, and dreams are much akin
To prayers; so her lips from time to time
Move silently.

While her hands stitch scraps
Of cloth, her heart still works upon the lives
She started years before and dares believe
They will be as strong and lovely as her quilt.

A patchwork of bright colors creates a a beautiful garden scene in this image by Superstock.

COLLECTOR'S CORNER

CHATELAINES AND ACCESSORIES

Laurie Hunter

We have only two young children in our home, but I can easily imagine how chaotic my grandmother's household must have been with nine children in a weathered farmhouse in east Texas. When Grandmother passed away, her few cherished possessions were dispersed among her children and grandchildren. I inherited an odd, bent, silver pin etched with an intricate design and a diminutive pair of tarnished sterling scissors whose blades measured no more than one inch. I wasn't sure why the miniature scissors, housed in a little dented case crowned with a tiny hook, were attached to the pin or what they had once been used for. But since they were tucked into Grandmother's cedar chest, along with a wedding-knot quilt, her father's pocket watch, photo albums, and other heirlooms, they must have been special to her.

I wondered what was so meaningful about the pin and its dangling scissors. Had they been given to Grandmother by a beau? Were they presents from her parents? In any case, there was no question about them being useless as they were—bent and tarnished. To honor the importance my grandmother had placed on the tokens, I took them to a jewelry shop to have them cleaned and repaired.

To my surprise the shop owner told me that the pin wasn't just a brooch and the pair of scissors certainly wasn't intended to be merely a costume jewelry bauble. The scissors had originally been an accessory on a chatelaine. "A what?" I quizzed. I learned that my pin was a chatelaine, a hook-like clasp typically worn at the waist or as a lapel ornament and used for suspending trinkets such as a watch, purse, needlecase, or keys. Interestingly, a chatelaine can also be defined as the mistress of a household or large establishment. Of course!

Grandmother had efficiently managed a household of nine children, three cats, and a dog, not to mention a husband. That certainly qualified as large. And she was surely never without a "fix-it" task to do. With her chatelaine clasping necessary tools of the trade onto her apron, she probably reached daily for the little scissors—to snip strings dangling off a hem, to open a parcel wrapped with twine, or to trim the hair of a young child who was forever looking unkempt.

What other "charms" had adorned her chatelaine? Though I'll never know, I now find great pleasure in seeking my own chatelaines and accessories from the same era. One silver chatelaine holds sewing-related items Grandmother probably would have enjoyed: an ivory needle case, a silver-plated thimble holder (tucked inside is a hand-painted, china thimble bearing the initial "G," for grandmother, I like to think), a sterling hook that may have been used for buttoning gloves or lacing shoes, and a miniature strawberry pin cushion topped with a green crushed-velvet stem. One chain remains empty; I'm saving it for a thimble case I've yet to find. My collection also includes a gorgeous chatelaine made entirely of salmon-colored silk ribbons suspending a tiny spool of thread, a pair of brass-handled scissors, and a silk bag containing spare celluloid buttons.

Though perfect for holding sewing tools, chatelaines were not limited to domestic use. I recently purchased a solid silver belt clip with a dog whistle dangling from one of its four chains; I'm sure a Victorian grandfather toted it on many turn-of-the-century hunting trips. I'm still looking for charms to attach to its other chains—maybe a pocket knife, or a spectacle case, or a notepad to record the day's success. I enjoy the search; that's half the fun, though I doubt Grandmother would agree. With nine children, I'm sure she spent much of her time scouring for one thing or another. But with her treasured chatelaine, perhaps Grandmother always knew where to find her sewing tools . . . just an arm's reach away.

SILVER THREADS AND GOLDEN NEEDLES

If you would like to collect chatelaines and related accessories, the following information may be helpful.

HISTORY

• Waist-hung items, predecessors to true chatelaines, date back to 2000 B.C.

• The earliest recorded mention of a chatelaine is in the April 1828 issue of *The World of Fashion.* Later issues state that chatelaines "are a very expensive article of jewelry" featuring gold buckles and chains.

• In the late eighteenth century, most chatelaines were fashioned from cut steel and were superior in workmanship and beauty to the chatelaines that were mass produced in the mid- and late-nineteenth century.

• As clothing styles began to change in the late nineteenth century, gowns made of heavy, layered fabrics were replaced with lighter, simpler dresses. In place of the heavy chatelaine pin, a finger ring was introduced to either be worn on the hand or looped over the belt of a dress.

• Though beauty of design was clearly a factor, a chatelaine's accessories were typically dictated by function. Ladies of the house, as well as craftsmen, artists, nurses, and others, were apt to carry tools unique to their trade.

• Chatelaines are intricately crafted pieces of history, representing the fashions, pastimes, trades, materials, and craftsmanship of a bygone era.

ADVICE FOR BEGINNING COLLECTORS

• Chatelaines with their original chains and accessories intact are the most valuable. It is not uncommon, however, for a chatelaine to be missing all of its original pieces due to loss or excessive wear.

• You may want to narrow your collection by searching for chatelaines and accessories that match your own style or profession. Or you can specialize in collecting chatelaines made from a particular material such as sterling silver or gold plate. Clasps can even be made from fabric, leather, or yarn.

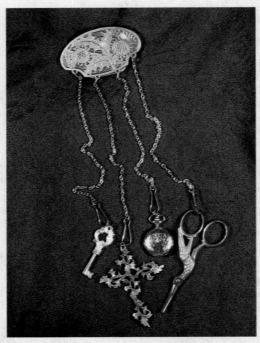

This silver chatelaine once kept a homemaker's necessities at her fingertips. Photo by James P. Rowan.

• If you want to collect sewing-related chatelaine accessories, look for thimbles, needlecases, pincushions, scissors, and tape measures. Other examples of chatelaine accessories not designed for sewing include pencils, notepads, purses, perfume bottles, knives, cases for glasses, and other handy tools.

• Be sure to keep a record of the pieces in your collection for future generations to appreciate and enjoy; note the piece's history, estimated date of manufacture, price, and sentimental value.

HOW TO CARE FOR YOUR CHATELAINES

• A chatelaine, like any heirloom, should be handled delicately. Cleaning and repairs should be done by a professional jeweler or craftsman.

• Once the pieces have been restored to their original condition, have your chatelaine collection cleaned only as needed. The less these delicate items are handled, the better.

• Store and display your collection in a velvet-lined viewing box or satin-lined envelope.

OLD MOTHERS

Charles Sarsfield Ross

I love old mothers—mothers with white hair
And kindly eyes and lips grown softly sweet
With murmured blessings over sleeping babes.
There is a something in their quiet grace
That speaks the calm of Sabbath afternoons;
A knowledge in their deep, unfaltering eyes
That far outreaches all philosophy.

Time, with caressing touch about them, weaves
The silver-threaded fairy-shawl of age,
While all the echoes of forgotten songs
Seem joined to lend a sweetness to their speech.
Old mothers—as they pass with slow-timed step,
Their trembling hands cling gently to youth's strength.
Sweet mothers—as they pass, one sees again
Old garden walks, old roses, and old loves.

Changeless

Isla Paschal Richardson

A mother's love is like the wondrous sun,
Yet in her heart love's day is never done.
Eternal, faithful, ceaselessly it lives.
A mother's love forever gives and gives.

Unselfishly this great love nothing asks,
Rejoicing in the many loving tasks
That fall to mother-hands, that fill her thought,
Her busy days with willing service fraught.

For all the countless things you've done for me,
For all the good that you have helped me see,
And for your love, as changeless as the light,
My thoughts and love go out to you tonight.

Journey

Author Unknown

She traveled the journey before you;
She has known all the cost of the way.
She paid out the price, to its fullness,
That motherhood only can pay.

She loved when the world was against you;
She hoped when your hope sank and died.
She clung to your hand when the clinging
Left scars in her heart, deep and wide.

She labored and loved and was happy,
For down deep in her kind heart she knew
Your kindness and love would repay her
For all that she did just for you.

*A Bible and bonnet rest among a few tender reminders of
Mother's love. Photo by Jessie Walker.*

THROUGH MY WINDOW

Pamela Kennedy

Art by Eve DeGrie

MOM'S BED AND BREAKFAST

Whoever said, "You can't go home again," certainly wasn't a college student! While our young adult offspring were anxious to take off for their destinations of higher learning, they seemed equally eager to return to the nest whenever the opportunity arose. Of course the fact that we now live in Hawaii might have something to do with it. We moved here the summer after our son completed his freshman year of college; and while we were still house hunting, he asked if he might invite a couple of his friends home for spring break the following year. "Sure," we responded, certain that whatever house we purchased could absorb a couple of college boys for a week.

Soon after classes started in the fall, our son called us to fill us in on his courses and how things were going. Then there was a slight pause in the conversation.

"Hey, Mom. Remember when I asked you if I could bring a couple of friends home for spring break?" I remembered. "Well, I guess I mentioned it to more people than I thought."

"How many are we talking about?" I responded, deciding I could probably absorb four boys instead of just the two I had planned on.

"If everybody can get tickets, there will be six, not counting me."

"Seven guys?" I tried to keep my tone even.

"Well, not exactly. Two are girls." He paused for a moment. "Mom, are you still there?"

As it turned out, one of the young ladies was particularly resourceful, and within two days the entire entourage had cut-rate tickets on a chartered airline flying out of Canada. Within a week, my husband's parents called and apprised us of the dates for their annual Hawaiian vacation. They planned to spend a week on Oahu before travelling to Maui for two additional weeks. Guess which week they'd be with us? Although they were willing to change their plans, their accommodations on the other island had already been booked and flight arrangements made. And, after all, once you've reached a certain point, what difference will two more make? Besides, they lived so far from all of us, it would be a great opportunity for them to meet some of their grandson's friends.

I began to strategize. Including my husband and myself, our daughter, the seven college kids, and two grandparents, our total occupancy was up to twelve. We have three bedrooms and two and a half bathrooms. By multiplying the number of daily meals by the number of showers, dividing them all by the amount of bedding required, and adding the square root of the vehicles needed to transport everyone, I arrived at the conclusion I needed a bottle of aspirin. Fortunately I had six months to plan.

By the time our guests started arriving, I felt a little bit like Henrietta Homemaker. My husband had cleaned out our double garage, lined up five cots, and turned it into a boys' dorm. Each cot was topped with a "Welcome to Hawaii" bundle created by my daughter containing a small bottle of beach sand, a cap, sunscreen, a keychain, and a small photo album. The grandparents were given our daughter's room, and she moved to the guest room, which became the girls' dorm, complete with bundles containing tote bags instead of hats. I had a

week's worth of menus posted on the fridge under the heading "Mother Kennedy's Home-Style Cookin'" and lots of fresh fruit, cereal, and bagels ready for the breakfast crowd. Early each morning I baked a batch of cookies which filled the kitchen with tantalizing aromas. They were usually gone by noon—as were the kids, headed for the beach or the mountains. My in-laws and I had plenty of time for leisurely conversations and second cups of coffee before they took an afternoon drive for shopping or sightseeing. Despite my earlier concerns, we never ran out of hot water, food, space, or good humor. The kids were wonderful guests, appreciative and happy to clean up after themselves; and my husband's parents were great sports, even to the point of treating all of us to a delightful spaghetti dinner at a local restaurant one evening.

The week sped by. There were only minor casualties: some sunburns and a few cuts from a fall on a mountain trail. The kids all had a memorable island vacation and left me with a touching note of thanks and a huge basket of treats. The grandparents went on to the rest of their holiday with delightful memories. As we folded up the cots and stowed the last of the extra bedding, my daughter reflected on the fun she had in joining her brother's friends on their excursions.

"I can hardly wait," she exclaimed while sweeping the last of the sand out of the garage, "until I can bring home six friends from college for spring break."

I went inside and poured myself a glass of iced tea. If I start tomorrow, I think I could be ready again in four years!

By multiplying the number of daily meals by the number of showers, dividing them all by the amount of bedding required, and adding the square root of the vehicles needed to transport everyone, I arrived at the conclusion I needed a bottle of aspirin.

Pamela Kennedy is a freelance writer of short stories, articles, essays, and children's books. Wife of a retired naval officer and mother of three children, she has made her home on both U.S. coasts and currently resides in Honolulu, Hawaii.

Carrot Cake
Nancy Pelosa of Albuquerque, New Mexico

2 cups granulated sugar
2 cups all-purpose flour
2 teaspoons ground cinnamon
1 teaspoon baking soda
1 teaspoon salt

1½ cups vegetable oil
4 eggs, beaten
3 cups grated carrots
1 8-ounce package cream cheese

¼ pound butter, softened
3½ cups powdered sugar
2 teaspoons vanilla
½ cup pecans

Preheat oven to 350° F. In a medium bowl, sift together sugar, flour, cinnamon, baking soda, and salt. Set aside. In a large bowl, combine oil, eggs, and carrots. Stir in dry ingredients by hand. Pour batter into a greased and floured, 9-by-13-inch baking dish. Bake 30 to 40 minutes or until a tooth-pick inserted in the middle comes out clean.

In a large bowl, combine all remaining ingredients except pecans. Blend until smooth. Spread icing over slightly cooled cake and top with ½ cup chopped pecans. Store in refrigerator. Makes 24 servings.

Black-Bottom Cupcakes
Grace Stephens of Bremerton, Washington

1 8-ounce package cream cheese
1 egg
1⅓ cups granulated sugar, divided
⅛ plus ½ teaspoon salt, divided

1 6-ounce package semisweet chocolate chips
1½ cups all-purpose flour
¼ cup cocoa
1 teaspoon baking soda

1 cup water
⅓ cup vegetable oil
1 tablespoon vinegar
1 teaspoon vanilla
Chopped walnuts

Preheat oven to 350° F. In a large bowl, combine cream cheese, egg, ⅓ cup sugar, and ⅛ teaspoon salt. Beat well. Stir in chocolate chips and set aside.

In a medium bowl, sift together flour, 1 cup sugar, cocoa, baking soda, and ½ teaspoon salt. Set aside. In a large bowl, com-bine water, oil, vinegar, and vanilla. Stir in dry ingredients. Mix well.

Line muffin pans with paper cups. Fill each cup ⅓ full with cocoa batter. Top with 1 heaping teaspoon cream cheese mixture. Sprinkle with walnuts. Bake 35 minutes. Makes 1 dozen cupcakes.

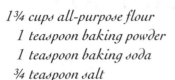

Coconut Oatmeal Cookies
Frances Radman of Cannon Falls, Minnesota

1¾ cups all-purpose flour
1 teaspoon baking powder
1 teaspoon baking soda
¾ teaspoon salt

1 cup granulated sugar
1 cup brown sugar
1 cup shortening
2 eggs

2 tablespoons vanilla
2 cups oats
2 cups flaked coconut

Preheat oven to 350° F. In a medium bowl, sift together first 4 ingredients. In a large bowl, cream together sugar, brown sugar, and shortening. Add eggs and vanilla. Beat well. Slowly stir in dry ingredients. Stir in oats and coconut. Shape dough into 1-inch balls and place on cookie sheet. Bake 15 to 17 minutes or until golden. Makes approximately 5 dozen cookies.

Chocolate Fudge
Julie Chan of Mississauga, Ontario

1 12-ounce package semisweet
   chocolate chips
¾ pound unsweetened chocolate

1 pint marshmallow cream
4½ cups granulated sugar
1 13-ounce can evaporated milk

2 tablespoons butter
2 tablespoons vanilla
2 cups chopped nuts

In a large bowl, combine chocolate chips, baking chocolate, and marshmallow cream; set aside. In a saucepan, combine sugar, milk, and butter. Boil 7 minutes, stirring occasionally. Add chocolate mixture; stir vigorously until chocolate is melted. Stir in vanilla. Fold in nuts. Turn batter into a buttered, 9-inch square baking dish. Let cool, then cut into pieces. Chill to keep firm. Makes 36 pieces.

Delicious Brownies
Marion Apgar of Coral Gables, Florida

1 package brownie mix
½ cup cocoa
⅔ cup semisweet chocolate chips

⅔ cup butterscotch chips
⅔ cup chopped nuts
18 large marshmallows

1 16-ounce container
   chocolate frosting

Preheat oven to 350° F. Prepare brownie batter according to package directions. Stir in cocoa, chocolate chips, butterscotch chips, and nuts. Pour into a 9-by-13-inch baking dish. Bake 15 minutes. Remove brownies from oven and arrange marshmallows evenly on top. Return to oven and bake an additional 12 to 15 minutes. Immediately spread melted marshmallows; top with frosting. Sprinkle with additional chocolate chips if desired. Run knife around edges while still warm. Chill before cutting. Makes 24 brownies.

ADVENTURE DRIVES WITH A GRANDSON

Isla Paschal Richardson

Adventure drives, we called them, you and I.
With bird book and field glasses, off we'd go
To find some nearby winding country road
"To see what we could see." All of six years,
You easily could spot the many birds
Whose names and songs we'd learned. We'd stop
By some clear stream and sail a boat we made
Of driftwood, with my handkerchief the sail.
We found field daisies, dug them by the roots;
And every spring in my backyard they bloomed,
And we'd recall the day I stepped in mud
And almost lost my shoe in reaching them.
And in the fall we'd gather hickory nuts
And ripe persimmons sweetened by the frost.
And once, do you remember how we splashed
Too hurriedly a swollen brook that crossed
The road—and drowned the engine? There we sat,
And I, not knowing what to do, talked on
Of how the trees clasped hands above the road—
And then a kind man came along and helped
Us out. Adventure drives! You saw a hawk
And solemnly declared you thought it was
An eagle. And we stopped to say good-day
To little lambs and pigs and baby goats.
We always found them on a certain road
In spring. . . . In junior high school now, of course
You have outgrown these drives. But still I hope
They stay in memory for you as bright
And sparkling-shiny as they do for me.

Inset: A grandmother and grandson hike through the meadows near the Cascade Mountains in Washington. Photo by John Terence Turner/FPG.

Right: A country road near Bridal Veil, Oregon, leads to adventure. Photo by Steve Terrill.

Path in the Grass

Grace Noll Crowell

This is the path worn bare by
    many feet:
My father's feet who sought his
    fields at dawn;
My mother, who would stop to
    smell the sweet
Wild clover blooming here, and
    then move on,
Helped make this small meander-
    ing path that goes
Its crooked way across the hills
    and down,
Arched here and there by fennel
    and wild rose;
Yet still the earth beneath lies
    packed and brown.

How many childhood mornings I
    have run
Along this path, my feet scarce
    touching ground;
The sweet, insistent wind, the
    caressing sun
Brushing my face, with only the
    lisping sound
Of grass and weeds as I went on
    swift wing
Helping create this lovely, lasting
    thing.

A well-worn path leads through the dew-covered lupine fields in Sugarhill, New Hampshire. Photo by Johnson's Photography.

Modern Miracle

Linda Healy

One spring day, our clothes dryer broke. Over twenty years old, it was beyond repair, and I hadn't the money to replace it right away.

"How did your mother do it?" my husband asked.

"That was the Middle Ages!" I said, remembering images of Mother and me dragging heavy baskets of wash to the backyard; shaking, shaking, shaking until the water soaked us; pinning sheets to the line while wet clothes flapped in our faces; hanging the clothes in the bathroom if it were a cold or rainy day and draping them over the radiators; then gathering it all and dragging out the ironing board for the day-long battle against wrinkles.

The laundromat was not an option. Money used on commercial dryers could be saved to buy a new dryer that much sooner.

"Middle Ages," I kept grumbling.

That first day I discovered how difficult it is to stretch a taut clothesline, how heavy a basket of wet clothes is, and how out-of-place a line of wash in the backyard looks nowadays. But I discovered something else as well.

As I put the last clothespin on a sheet and turned to grab the next item from the basket, I found myself caught between two sheets. The view of my own and neighboring yards was cut off. In my tiny, timeless cocoon, long-forgotten memories stirred, memories of Mother and me hanging the wash and talking. She told me about how her mother, who still lived in Ukraine, brushed and braided my mother's hair every morning, how their tiny house had been always full of the rich smell of fresh bread, how her mother's eyes lit up whenever Mother brought the school history book home to read aloud. Through these stories, Grandmother, whom I had never met, came alive for me.

And I told Mother about a painting I had done in school that the teacher hung on the hall outside our classroom, and Mother's proud smile felt warmer than the sunshine.

Mother told me about her first job as a court stenographer in a small village in Ukraine, how she invented her own form of shorthand, and how satisfied she was to do work that she enjoyed.

I told her about the cute boy who sat next to me in class and the friendly notes he passed to me when the teacher wasn't looking. I loved the gentle understanding in Mother's eyes as I spoke.

We never talked as much as we did on wash day. And it was always a surprise when I reached into the basket and found it empty.

Back in the present day, standing between the fluttering sheets, I heard sly footsteps in the grass. Moments later, small hands raised a sheet, and an elfin face peeked under it.

"Boo!"

I pretended to be frightened.

My young son, a late-life blessing, beamed at me. "Whatcha doin', Mom?"

"Playing a game," I said. "Want to join me?"

He edged in between the sheets to stand beside me. "Oh! It's like a fort!"

"Yes. And the pirates are surrounding us so we have to build more walls."

"Well, hurry, Mom." He grabbed something from the basket and handed it to me.

A bird called from a nearby tree.

"That's the pirates' secret code," my son whispered. "They're planning to surprise us from the rear, I think."

"Dad's t-shirt should block them pretty well."

"It's not a t-shirt, Mom. It's a log."

"Of course."

Only two or three items remained in the basket when my husband appeared, carrying a tray with a pitcher of lemonade and three glasses on it.

"What's all the laughing and hollering?" he asked.

"We're protecting our fort from the pirates," our son said.

"On the way through the forest," my husband said, "I saw them settling down for lunch. I think it's safe for us to take a break."

We all sat down beneath the wash and sipped lemonade and talked. And talked. We never talked

Artist Robert Spencer captures a sunny day of chores in Woman Hanging Clothes. *Image from Christie's Images.*

so much as we did that sunny afternoon. Just like my mother and I had done on wash day.

By September, we had saved enough to buy a new dryer. But the weather was still balmy, so I pre-

tended the money wasn't there. After all, the "Middle Ages" had their good points too, and sharing a weekly adventure and conversation with my family was worth the trip back in time.

Vintage House

John Ransom Lewis

Old houses
have a way of living longer
in a small town.
An old house rarely loses
its identity.
It has a personality
all its own.
It's recognized—
it has friends—

Little boys
know the peepholes
where the shutters are cracked
and saggy—
and flick a few more pieces
of peeling paint
off the corners
each time they pass.

Little girls
look longingly
ladylike
through the front door panes
at dusty chandeliers and musty drapes
and rock
their unborn memories
in the battered rocker
aimed at the front walk.

It's nice to have friends!
Especially
as you grow old.

A vintage house stands among the flowers in GARDEN
RETREAT *by artist Dwayne Warwick. Image copyright ©
Arts Uniq, Inc., Cookeville, Tennessee.*

LILACS FOR MEMORIAL DAY

Rose Koralewsky

The lush grass deepens by forgotten roads
Where little vagrant breezes softly stray,
Laden with fragrance from the leafy bowers
Where blossom lilacs for Memorial Day.

The dewy sprays of Tyrian rose and white
Still nod above the stone walls old and gray,
As once when happy children laughed with joy
To see the lilacs for Memorial Day.

Gone are the ancient houses mossy-roofed,
Gone the white schoolhouse where in brave array
The bright-eyed boys and girls once proudly marched,
Bearing their lilacs for Memorial Day.

The volleys and the bugle notes are stilled,
And bright flags flutter in the sun's last ray;
Once more they bloom on fair New England hills—
The hallowed lilacs for Memorial Day.

Lilac blossoms crown a bush in Ringwood, New Jersey.
Photo by Gene Ahrens.

Blessing on a Garden

Nancy Byrd Turner

Come, all good birds!
Robin and wren and thrush,
For every one a bush—
Come with glad words.

And all bright flowers:
Phlox and delphinium,
Rose and tall lily, come—
Make fair the hours.

Come, bees, because here
Sweets without measure
Wait for your pleasure.
Butterflies, pause here.

Toads, find you room.
In the sweet thickets,
Humble brown crickets,
Make you a home.

Be kind here, weather!
Rain, wet the tender roots;
Sun, warm the golden fruits;
Dews, softly gather.

Love, be the warden;
Peace, all the borders fold.
God Himself once of old
Walked in a garden.

A water garden in Floyds Knobs, Indiana, serves as home to frogs and flowers. Photo by Daniel Dempster.

Cradle in the Willow

Amelia Evans Mix

In its youth one branch of the tree was bent
And trampled in the mud to root and grow,
Where it blended in with the mother tree
At the edge of the pond not too long ago.

In the spring I watched the singing courtship
Of some kingbirds high on a quivering bough;
One day I found they had started nesting
Where the bent branch subtly would allow.

There the wind waltzed across the water
And danced the leaves on the willow tree
Where it stooped to bend low the tall pond grasses;
And the arrowhead lilies nodded to me.

Oh, to hatch in a nest built in a willow!
To hear the wind whisper enchantingly!
To sleep in a nest out over the water
On the low-flung branch of a willow tree.

*Spring hangs her infant blossoms on the trees,
Rocked in the cradle of the western breeze.*
—*William Cowper*

A stately willow drapes over the pond in the Royal Botanical Gardens in Hamilton, Ontario. Photo by Gene Ahrens.

THE MUSIC FROM THE HILLS

Come walk with me this morning of sun, and we'll make it a walk through the year, a year of never-ending music from the hills. The music may change, but it never ends.

From one May to the next come the chorus of birds, the heavy rolling drums of a summer thundershower, the liquid song of streams flowing down the hills, the dripping of rain on rooftop and leaf, the peeper's rhythmic chords from April swamps, the summer orchestra of katydids and crickets, the evening organ-roll of the thrush. I take the music as it comes with each season of the year. I am delighted by the changes from one season to the next, from the whispering breezes to the gusts and gales, from a bluebird's warble to a chipmunk's tremolo.

There is love and there is peace in what I hear. There is tranquility in the way nature unfolds its seasons of music. I always find that I am in step with the year, and the pace is good. I can smile with the hills, and I can meditate. I can chant with the seasons' flowing rhythms, and I can dream.

The year is preparing now to open the door to summer to take the place of spring. The music will change; but when one great recording slows and ebbs with a waning season, another takes its place with a joyous beginning.

Throughout the year there is no finale. There are placid chords and surging notes. There is joy and sweet serenity. Nature's music flows in the fleeting footsteps of the years. So I walk with her, hand in hand, and I listen to the music from the hills.

The author of three books, Lansing Christman has contributed to Ideals *for almost thirty years. Mr. Christman has also been published in several American, foreign, and braille anthologies. He lives in rural South Carolina.*

A stream rushes past the wildflowers in Alberta, Canada. Photo by Alan Kearney/FPG.

Come Slowly, Summer

L. Eleanor Voswinkel

Come slowly, summer, not with undue speed,
That we may hold each cherished sign of spring
In outstretched hands and lovingly take heed
Of bird and bee forever on the wing;
Of meadowlarks who joyously now spill
Their cadenced music from each throbbing throat;
While sugar maples, on a distant hill,
Half blurred and dim, in roseate ether float.

Come slowly, summer, fill each heart with peace.
The ice-locked stream leaps forth in wild delight;
Breaking its bounds, it swirls in swift release
From winter's tomb, rejoicing in its might.
Come slowly, summer, and let each heart declare,
"God's in His heaven. All His works are fair."

*Left: Spring-flowering balsam root joins the purple lupine in
Oregon's Columbia Gorge National Scenic Area.
Photo by Mary Liz Austin.
Border: Grace Ward carpets the ground in Multnomah
County, Oregon. Photo by Steve Terrill.*

Readers' Forum

Snapshots from Our Ideals Readers

Top left: Dakotah Katherine Boone shows her affinity for a lovely field of bluebonnets, the state flower of her home state of Texas. The picture was sent to us by proud grandmother Anna-Marie Mozzicato of Ft. Myers, Florida. Anna-Marie tells us that she and her husband, Frank, have scanned Dakotah's picture onto their computer's desktop so that the couple can start each day with a smile.

Lower left: Darrin and Leigh Anne Rowe of Limestone, Tennessee, share this delightful photo of eight-month-old Addisyn Perrette Rowe, whom they like to say will "bloom where she is planted." Addisyn has two older brothers, Dale Rowe and Colton Scott Rowe, who are the other treasures in their family's "field of blooms"!

Top right: From Manheim, Pennsylvania, Edna Mast sends this snapshot of her great-granddaughter, Julia Nolt. Little Julia is happily nestled in a bed of posies at her home near Harrisonburg, Virginia. Edna tells us that Julia is a friend of flowers and loves being outdoors among them.

Top right: Not only is Ariel Morningstarr of Mansfield, Ohio, lucky enough to live only a block from the beautiful gardens at Kingwood Center, but she has a four-year-old grandson who loves to explore the gardens with her. Heath Evan Christian poses here before a backdrop of roses.

Top left: Juanita McCreight of Ellsworth, Kansas, tells us that her grandson, William McCreight, enjoys helping his mother tend the garden and believes his job of watering the flowers to be serious business. Juanita tells us that it is a joy to watch young William being helpful.

THANK YOU Anna-Marie Mozzicato, Darrin and Leigh Anne Rowe, Edna Mast, Ariel Morningstarr, Juanita McCreight, Don and Dorothy Jimison, and Francenia Patterson for sharing your family photographs with *Ideals.* We hope to hear from other readers who would like to share snapshots with the *Ideals* family. Please include a self-addressed, stamped envelope if you would like the photos returned. Keep your original photographs for safekeeping and send duplicate photos along with your name, address, and telephone number to:

Readers' Forum
Ideals Publications
535 Metroplex Drive, Suite 250
Nashville, Tennessee 37211

Above: It is clear to see how two-year-old Lucy Jimison earned the nickname "Lucy the Princess." Lucy is the granddaughter of Don and Dorothy Jimison of Appomattox, Virginia, and makes her home in Temple, Texas.

Dear *Ideals*,

I enjoy your publication very much and enjoy the pictures of children. In looking through some of mine, here is one I'd love to share of our only grandchild, little Bethany Lee Russell *(pictured at right)*. She and I attended a dress-up tea party and storytime when she was only eighteen months old. She is almost four years old now, but still loves to dress up and go to church, to Nanny's house, and to special events like vacation Bible school. We are very proud of her, and she brightens our lives daily.

Francenia Patterson
Pulaski, Tennessee

ideals

Publisher, Patricia A. Pingry
Editor, Michelle Prater Burke
Designer, Travis Rader
Copy Editor, Elizabeth Kea
Editorial Assistant, Amy Johnson
Contributing Editors, Lansing Christman, Pamela Kennedy, Nancy Skarmeas, and Lisa Ragan

ACKNOWLEDGMENTS

CROWELL, GRACE NOLL. "Path in the Grass" from *Bright Harvest.* Copyright © 1952 by Grace Noll Crowell. Published by arrangement with HarperCollins Publishers, Inc. All rights reserved. GUEST, EDGAR A. "Dressing Up" from *All in a Lifetime.* Used by permission of the author's estate. HOLMES, MARJORIE. An excerpt from "The Kites and Rites of Spring" from *You and I and Yesterday.* Used by permission of the author. KORALEWSKY, ROSE. "Lilacs for Memorial Day" from *New England Heritage and Other Poems.* Used by permission of Branden Publishing. RICHARDSON, ISLA PASCHAL. "Adventure Drives with a Grandson" from *Against All Time* and "Heart-Beats" from *My Heart Waketh.* Used by permission of Branden Publishing. STRONG, PATIENCE. "Sticky Fingers" from *Morning Glory.* Copyright © 1958 by Patience Strong. Reprinted by permission of Rupert Crew Limited. Our sincere thanks to the following authors whom we were unable to locate: John Ransom Lewis for "Vintage House"; Mary O'Connor for "Spring"; Nancy Byrd Turner for "Blessing on a Garden"; L. Eleanor Voswinkel for "Come Slowly, Summer."

Sweet Spring
Frieda Hawes

Sweet spring, attired in white-winged bliss,
When I knew sunshine's ever rapturous kiss,
When breezes tagged new grass in turbulent play
And buds unfolded to the warmth of May.

The house up in a tree, the lumber mill,
A curling thread of smoke atop a hill—
How often have I stood in broomsage field
To marvel at the season's bumper yield!

Sweet hours of nature at my feet
When each new day held magic so complete;
How often have I known, remembering
The blessed hours of one allotted spring!

Memories
Mildred M. North

Again the lilac blossoms sway
Above the windowsills,
And every white or purple spray
Exotic perfume spills.

Again the orchard rows are sweet
With drifts of blossom snow,
And every breath of fragrance fleet
Brings thoughts of long ago.

So clear, so precious, memory sees
The old home, Mother dear,
And lilac blooms and apple trees—
The joys of yesteryear.

A hillside in Clackamas County, Oregon, is crowned with foxglove and lupine. Photo by Steve Terrill.

The Spousal Time of May

Coventry Patmore

'Twas when the spousal time of May
Hangs all the hedge with bridal wreaths,
And air's so sweet the bosom gay
Gives thanks for every breath it breathes;
When like to like is gladly moved,
And each thing joins in spring's refrain,
"Let those love now who never loved;
Let those who have loved love again";
That I, in whom the sweet time wrought,
Lay stretch'd within a lonely glade,
Abandon'd to delicious thought,
Beneath the softly twinkling shade.
The leaves, all stirring, mimick'd well
A neighboring rush of rivers cold,
And as the sun or shadow fell,
So these were green and those were gold.
In dim recesses hyacinths drooped,
And breadths of primrose lit the air,
Which, wandering through the
        woodland, stooped
And gathered perfumes here and there.
Upon the spray the squirrel swung,
And careless songsters, six or seven,
Sang lofty songs the leaves among,
Fit for their only listener, Heaven.

When April steps aside for May,
Like diamonds all the raindrops glisten;
Fresh violets open every day:
To some new bird each hour we listen.
                                   —Lucy Larcom

ideals®
MOTHER'S DAY

More Than 50 Years of Celebrating Life's Most Treasured Moments

Vol. 58, No. 2

It was a glorious May morning, Tingling with the joy of life.
—*Melvin B. Tolson*

Featured Photograph
6

Readers' Reflections
28

Collector's Corner
58

Bits and Pieces
8

Devotions from
the Heart
33

Through My Window
64

Remember When
12

A Slice of Life
36

Ideals' Family
Recipes
66

From My
Garden Journal
16

Handmade Heirloom
48

Country Chronicle
82

For the Children
20

Legendary Americans
50

Readers' Forum
86

Traveler's Diary
54

IDEALS—Vol. 58, No. 2 March MMI IDEALS (ISSN 0019-137X, USPS 256-240)
is published six times a year: January, March, May, July, September, and November by
IDEALS PUBLICATIONS, a division of Guideposts
39 Seminary Hill Road, Carmel, NY 10512.
Copyright © MMI by IDEALS PUBLICATIONS, a division of Guideposts.
All rights reserved. The cover and entire contents of IDEALS are fully protected by copyright
and must not be reproduced in any manner whatsoever.
Title IDEALS registered U.S. Patent Office. Printed and bound in USA by Quebecor Printing.

Printed on Weyerhaeuser Husky. The paper used in this publication meets the minimum requirements of
American National Standard for Information Sciences—
Permanence of Paper for Printed Library Materials, ANSI Z39.48-1984.

Periodicals postage paid at Carmel, New York, and additional mailing offices.
POSTMASTER: Send address changes to Ideals, 39 Seminary Hill Road, Carmel, NY 10512.
For subscription or customer service questions, contact Ideals Publications,
a division of Guideposts, 39 Seminary Hill Road, Carmel, NY 10512. Fax 845-228-2115.

Reader Preference Service: We occasionally make our mailing lists available to
other companies whose products or services might interest you.
If you prefer not to be included, please write to Ideals Customer Service.

ISBN 0-8249-1166-0 GST 893989236

Visit *Ideals*'s website at www.idealspublications.com

Cover
Spring Blossoms
Nancy Matthews,
Photographer

Inside Front Cover
MINDY'S PEONIES
Kim McDevitt, Artist
Image from Kim Sailers/
Superstock

Inside B
SPRING
Edwin B
Haynes Fine A
Galleries. Fine A
Library, London/A

D1315219